# DIVINE LITURGY OF ST. MARK

**Translated by:** James Donaldson
**Edited by:** D.P. Curtin

Dalcassian
Publishing
Company

PHILADELPHIA, PA

Translated by James Donaldson. From Ante-Nicene Fathers, Vol. 7. Edited by
Alexander Roberts, James Donaldson, and A. Cleveland Coxe. (Buffalo, NY:
Christian Literature Publishing Co., 1886.)

Library of Congress Cataloging-in-Publication Data

# 1

*The Divine Liturgy of the Holy Apostle and Evangelist Mark, The Disciple of the Holy Peter.*

*The Priest.*

I. Peace be to all.

*The People.*

And to your spirit.

*The Deacon.*

Pray.

*The People.*

Lord, have mercy; Lord, have mercy; Lord, have mercy.

*The Priest prays secretly:*

We give You thanks, yea, more than thanks, O Lord our God, the Father of our Lord and God and Saviour Jesus Christ, for all Your goodness at all times and in all places, because You have shielded, rescued, helped, and guided us all the days of our lives, and brought us unto this hour, permitting us again to stand before You in Your holy place, that we may implore forgiveness of our sins and propitiation to all Your people. We pray and beseech You, merciful God, to grant in Your goodness that we may spend this holy day and all the time of our lives without sin, in fullness of joy, health, safety, holiness, and reverence of You. But all envy, all fear, all temptation, all the influence of Satan, all the snares of wicked men, do You, O Lord, drive away from us, and from Your Holy Catholic and Apostolic Church. Bestow upon us, O Lord, what is good and meet. Whatever sin we commit in thought, word, or deed, do You in Your goodness and mercy be pleased to pardon. Leave us not, O Lord, while we hope in You; nor lead us into temptation, but deliver us from the evil one and from his works, through the grace, mercy, and love of Your only-begotten Son.

( *In a loud voice.*)

Through whom and with whom be glory and power to You, in Your most holy, good, and life-giving Spirit, now, henceforth, and for evermore.

*The People.*

Amen.

*The Priest.*

II. Peace be to all.

*The People.*

And to your spirit.

*The Deacon.*

Pray for the king.

*The People.*

Lord, have mercy; Lord, have mercy; Lord, have mercy.

*The Priest prays.*

O God, Sovereign Lord, the Father of our Lord and God and Saviour Jesus Christ, we pray and beseech You to grant that our king may enjoy peace, and be just and brave. Subdue under him, O God, all his adversaries and enemies. Gird on your shield and armour, and rise to his aid. Give him the victory, O God, that his heart may be set on peace and the praise of Your holy name, that we too in his peaceful reign may spend a calm and tranquil life in all reverence and godly fear, through the grace, mercy, and love of Your only-begotten Son:

( *In a loud voice.*)

Through whom and with whom be glory and power to You, with Your most holy, good, and life-giving Spirit, now, henceforth, and for evermore.

*The People.*

Amen.

*The Priest.*

III. Peace be to all.

*The People.*

And to your spirit.

*The Deacon.*

Pray for the papas and the bishop.

*The People.*

Lord, have mercy; Lord, have mercy; Lord, have mercy.

*The Priest.*

O Sovereign and Almighty God, the Father of our Lord, God, and Saviour Jesus Christ, we pray and beseech You to defend in Your good mercy our most holy and blessed high priest our Father in God Δ, and our most reverend Bishop Δ . Preserve them for us through many years in peace, while they according to Your holy and blessed will fulfil the sacred priesthood committed to their care, and dispense aright the word of truth; with all the orthodox bishops, elders, deacons, sub-deacons, readers, singers, and laity, with the entire body of the Holy and only Catholic Church. Graciously bestow upon them peace, health, and salvation. The prayers they offer up for us, and we for them, do You, O Lord, receive at Your holy, heavenly, and reasonable altar. But all the enemies of Your Holy Church put speedily under their feet, through the grace, mercy, and love of Your only-begotten Son:

*(Aloud.)*

Through whom and with whom be glory and power to You, with Your all-holy, good, and life-giving Spirit, now, henceforth, and for evermore.

*The People.*

Amen.

*The Priest.*

IV. Peace be to all.

*The People.*

And to your spirit.

*The Deacon.*

Stand and pray.

*The People.*

Lord have mercy (thrice).

*The Priest offers up the prayer of entrance, and for incense.*

*The Priest.*

O Sovereign Lord our God, who hast chosen the lamp of the twelve apostles with its twelve lights, and hast sent them forth to proclaim throughout the whole world and teach the Gospel of Your kingdom, and to heal sickness and every weakness among the people, and hast breathed upon their faces and said unto them, Receive the Holy Spirit the Comforter: whosoever sins you remit, they are remitted unto them; and whosoever sins you retain, they are retained: Breathe also Your Holy Spirit upon us Your servants, who, standing around, are about to enter on Your holy service, upon the bishops, elders, deacons, readers, singers, and laity, with the entire body of the Holy Catholic and Apostolic Church.

From the curse and execration, from condemnation, imprisonment, and banishment, and from the portion of the adversary;

O Lord, deliver us.

Purify our lives and cleanse our hearts from all pollution and from all wickedness, that with pure heart and conscience we may offer to You this incense for a sweet-smelling savour, and for the remission of our sins and the sins of all Your people, through the grace, mercy, and love of Your only-begotten Son:

*(Aloud.)*

Through whom and with whom be the glory and the power to You, with Your all-holy, good, and life-giving Spirit, now, henceforth, and for evermore.

*The People.*

Amen.

*The Deacon.*

V. Stand.

*They sing:—*

Only-begotten Son and Word, etc.

*The Gospel is carried in, and the Deacon says:—*

Let us pray.

*The Priest.*

Peace be to all.

*The People.*

And to your spirit.

*The Deacon.*

Let us pray.

*The People.*

Lord, have mercy.

*The Priest says the prayer of the Trisagion.*

O Sovereign Lord Christ Jesus, the co-eternal Word of the eternal Father, who was made in all things like as we are, but without sin, for the salvation of our race; who hast sent forth Your holy disciples and apostles to proclaim and teach the Gospel of Your kingdom, and to heal all disease, all sickness among Your people, be pleased now, O Lord, to send forth Your light and Your truth. Enlighten the eyes of our minds, that we may understand Your divine oracles. Fit us to become hearers, and not only hearers, but doers of Your word, that we, becoming fruitful, and yielding good fruit from thirty to an hundred fold, may be deemed worthy of the kingdom of heaven.

*(Aloud.)*

Let Your mercy speedily overtake us, O Lord. For You are the bringer of good tidings, the Saviour and Guardian of our souls and bodies; and we offer glory, thanks, and the *Trisagion* to You, the Father, Son, and Holy Ghost, now, henceforth, and for evermore.

*The People.*

Amen. Holy God, holy mighty, holy immortal. Holy, holy, holy, etc.

*VI. After the Trisagion the Priest makes the sign of the cross over the people, and says:—*

Peace be to all.

*The People.*

And to your spirit.

*Then follow the Let us attend; The Apostle and Prologue of the Hallelujah. The Deacons, after a prescribed form, say:—*

Lord, bless us.

*The Priest says:—*

May the Lord in His mercy bless and help us, now, henceforth, and for evermore.

*The Priest, before the Gospel is read, offers incense, and says:—*

Accept at Your holy, heavenly, and reasonable altar, O Lord, the incense we offer in presence of Your sacred glory. Send down upon us in return the grace of Your Holy Spirit, for You are blessed, and let Your glory encircle us.

*VII. The Deacon, when he is about to read the Gospel, says:—*

Lord, bless us.

*The Priest.*

May the Lord, who is the blessed God, bless and strengthen us, and make us hearers of His holy Gospel, now, henceforth, and for evermore. Amen.

*The Deacon.*

Stand and let us hear the holy Gospel.

*The Priest.*

Peace be to all.

*The People.*

And to your spirit.

*VIII. The Deacon reads the Gospel, and the Priest says the prayer of the Collect.*

Look down in mercy and compassion, O Lord, and heal the sick among Your people.

May all our brethren who have gone or who are about to go abroad, safely reach their destination in due season.

Send down the gracious rain upon the thirsty lands, and make the rivers flow in full stream, according to Your grace.

The fruits of the land do You, O Lord, fill with seed and make ripe for the harvest.

In peace, courage, justice, and tranquillity preserve the kingdom of Your servant, whom You have deemed worthy to reign over this land.

From evil days, from famine and pestilence, from the assault of barbarians, defend, O Lord, this Christ-loving city, lowly and worthy of Your compassion, as You spared Nineveh of old.

For You are full of mercy and compassion, and rememberest not the iniquities of men against them.

You have said through Your prophet Isaiah,— I will defend this city, to save it for my own sake, and for my servant David's sake.

Wherefore we pray and beseech You to defend in Your good mercy this city, for the sake of the martyr and evangelist Mark, who has shown us the way of salvation through the grace, mercy, and love of Your only-begotten Son.

*(Aloud.)*

Through whom and with whom be glory and power to You, with Your all-holy, good, and life-giving Spirit.

*The Deacon.*

IX. Begin.

*Then they say the verse. The Deacon says— The three.*

*The Priest.*

O Sovereign and Almighty God, the Father of our Lord Jesus Christ, we pray and beseech You to fill our hearts with the peace of heaven, and to bestow moreover the peace of this life. Preserve for us through many years our most holy and blessed *Papas* Δ, and our most pious Bishop Δ, while they, according to Your holy and blessed will, peacefully fulfil the holy priesthood committed to their care, and dispense aright the word of truth, with all the orthodox bishops, elders, deacons, sub-deacons, readers, singers, with the entire body of the holy Catholic and Apostolic Church. Bless our meetings, O Lord. Grant that we may hold them without let or hindrance, according to Your holy will. Be pleased to give to us, and Your servants after us for ever, houses of praise and prayer. Rise, O Lord, and let Your enemies be scattered. Let all who hate Your holy name be put to flight. Bless Your faithful and orthodox people. Multiply them by thousands and tens of thousands. Let no deadly sin prevail against them, or against Your holy people, through the grace, mercy, and love of Your only-begotten Son.

*( Aloud.)*

Through whom and with whom be glory and power to You, with Your all-holy, good, and life-giving Spirit.

*The People.*

Amen.

*The Priest.*

Peace be to all.

*The People.*

And to your spirit.

*The Deacon.*

Take care that none of the catechumens —

# 2

*Then they sing the Cherubic hymn.*

*X. The Priest offers incense at the entrance, and prays:—*

O Lord our God, who lackest nothing, accept this incense offered by an unworthy hand, and deem us all worthy of Your blessing, for You are our sanctification, and we ascribe glory to You.

*The holy things are carried to the altar, and the Priest prays thus:—*

O holy, highest, awe-inspiring God, who dwellest among the saints, sanctify us, and deem us worthy of Your reverend priesthood. Bring us to Your precious altar with a good conscience, and cleanse our hearts from all pollution. Drive away from us all unholy thoughts, and sanctify our souls and minds. Grant that, with reverence of You, we may perform the service of our holy fathers, and propitiate Your presence through all time; for You are He who blesses and sanctifies all things, and to You we ascribe glory and thanks.

*The Deacon.*

XI. Salute one another.

*The Priest says the prayer of salutation.*

O Sovereign and Almighty Lord, look down from heaven on Your Church, on all Your people, and on all Your flock. Save us all, Your unworthy servants, the sheep of Your fold. Give us Your peace, Your help, and Your love, and send to us the gift of Your Holy Spirit, that with a pure heart and a good conscience we may salute one another with an holy kiss, without hypocrisy, and with no hostile purpose, but guileless and pure in one spirit, in the bond of peace and love, one body and one spirit, in one faith, even as we have been called in one hope of our calling, that we may all meet in the divine and boundless love, in Christ Jesus our Lord, with whom You are blessed.

*Then the Priest offers the incense, and says:—*

The incense is offered to Your name. Let it ascend, we implore You, from the hands of Your poor and sinful servants to Your heavenly altar for a sweet-smelling savour, and the propitiation of all Your people. For all glory, honour, adoration, and thanks are due unto You, the Father, Son, and Holy Ghost, now, henceforth, and for evermore. Amen.

*After the Salutation, the Deacon in a loud voice says:—*

XII. Stand and make the offering duly.

*The Priest, making the sign of the cross over the disks and chalices, says in a loud voice (the Nicene Creed):—*

I believe in one God, etc.

*The Deacon.*

Stand for prayer.

*The Priest.*

Peace be to all.

*The Deacon.*

Pray for those who present the offering.

*The Priest says the prayer of the Oblation.*

O Sovereign Lord, Christ Jesus the Word, who art equal in power with the Father and the Holy Spirit, the great high priest; the bread that came down from heaven, and saved our souls from ruin; who gavest Yourself, a spotless Lamb, for the life of the world....

We pray and beseech You, O Lord, in Your mercy, to let Your presence rest upon this bread and these chalices on the all-holy table, while angels, archangels, and Your holy priests stand round and minister for Your glory and the renewing of our souls, through the grace, mercy, and love of Your only-begotten Son, through whom and with whom be glory and power to You.

*And when the People say,*

And from the Holy Spirit was He made flesh;

*The Priest makes the sign of the cross, and says:—*

And was crucified for us.

*The Priest makes the sign of the cross again, and says:—*

And to the Holy Spirit.

# 3

*XIII. In like manner also, as after the Creed, he makes the sign of the cross upon the People, and says aloud:—*

The Lord be with all.

*The People.*

And with your spirit.

*The Priest.*

Let us lift up our hearts.

*The People.*

We lift them up to the Lord.

*The Priest.*

Let us give thanks to the Lord.

*The People.*

It is meet and right.

*The Priest begins the Anaphoral prayer.*

O Lord God, Sovereign and Almighty Father, truly it is meet and right, holy and becoming, and good for our souls, to praise, bless, and thank You; to make open confession to You by day and night with voice, lips, and heart without ceasing;

To You who hast made the heaven, and all that is therein; the earth, and all that is therein; The sea, fountains, rivers, lakes, and all that is therein;

To You who, after Your own image and likeness, has made man, upon whom You also bestowed the joys of Paradise;

And when he trespassed against You, You neither neglected nor forsook him, good Lord,

But recalled him by Your law, instruct him by Your prophets, restore and renew him by this awful, life-giving, and heavenly mystery.

And all this You have done by Your Wisdom and the Light of truth, Your only-begotten Son, our Lord, God, and Saviour Jesus Christ, Through whom, thanking You with Him and the Holy Spirit,

We offer this reasonable and bloodless sacrifice, which all nations, from the rising to the setting of the sun, from the north and the south, present to You, O Lord; for great is Your name among all peoples, and in all places are incense, sacrifice, and oblation offered to Your holy name.

XIV. We pray and beseech You, O lover of men, O good Lord, remember in Your good mercy the Holy and only Catholic and Apostolic Church throughout the whole world, and all Your people, and all the sheep of this fold. Vouchsafe to the hearts of all of us the peace of heaven, but grant us also the peace of this life.

Guide and direct in all peace the king, army, magistrates, councils, peoples, and neighbourhoods, and all our outgoings and incomings.

O King of Peace, grant us Your peace in unity and love. May we be Yours, O Lord; for we know no other God but You, and name no other name but Yours. Give life unto the souls of all of us, and let no deadly sin prevail against us, or against all Your people.

Look down in mercy and compassion, O Lord, and heal the sick among Your people. Deliver them and us, O Lord, from sickness and disease, and drive away the spirit of weakness.

Raise up those who have been long afflicted, and heal those who are vexed with unclean spirits.

Have mercy on all who are in prison, or in mines, or on trial, or condemned, or in exile, or crushed by cruel bondage or tribute. Deliver them, O Lord, for You are our God, who settest the captives free; who raisest up the downtrodden; who givest hope to the hopeless, and help to the helpless; who liftest up the fallen; who givest refuge to the shipwrecked, and vengeance to the oppressed.

Pity, relieve, and restore every Christian soul that is afflicted or wandering.

But You, O Lord — the physician of our souls and bodies, the guardian of all flesh — look down, and by Your saving power heal all the diseases of soul and body.

Guide and prosper our brethren who have gone or who are about to go abroad. Whether they travel by land, or river, or lake, by public road, or in whatever way journeying, bring them everywhere to a safe and tranquil haven. Be pleased to be with them by land and sea, and restore them in health and joy to joyful and healthful homes.

Ever defend, O Lord, our journey through this life from trouble and storm.

Send down rich and copious showers on the dry and thirsty lands.

Gladden and revive the face of the earth, that it may spring forth and rejoice in the raindrops.

Make the waters of the river flow in full stream.

Gladden and revive the face of the earth with the swelling waters.

Fill all the channels of the streams, and multiply the fruits of the earth.

Bless, O Lord, the fruits of the earth, and keep them safe and unharmed. Fill them with seed, and make them ripe for the harvest.

Bless even now, O Lord, Your yearly crown of blessing for the sake of the poor of Your people, the widow, the orphan, and the stranger, and for the sake of all of us who have our hope in You and call upon Your holy name; for the eyes of all are upon You, and You give them bread in due season.

O You who gives food to all flesh, fill our hearts with joy and gladness, that at all times, having all sufficiency, we may abound to every good work in Christ Jesus our Lord.

O King of kings and Lord of lords, defend the kingdom of Your servant, our orthodox and Christ-loving sovereign, whom You have deemed worthy to reign over this land in peace, courage, and justice.

Subdue under him, O Lord, every enemy and adversary, whether at home or abroad. Gird on Your shield and armour, and rise to his aid. Draw Your sword, and help him to fight against them that persecute him. Shield him in the day of battle, and grant that the fruit of his loins may sit upon his throne.

Be kind to him, O Lord, for the sake of Your Holy and Apostolic Church, and all Your Christ-loving people, that we too in his peaceful reign may live a calm and tranquil life, in all reverence and godliness.

O Lord our God, give peace to the souls of our fathers and brethren who have fallen asleep in Jesus, remembering our forefathers of old, our fathers, patriarchs, prophets, apostles, martyrs, confessors, bishops, and the souls of all the holy and just men who have died in the Lord.

Especially remember those whose memory we this day celebrate, and our holy father Mark, the apostle and evangelist, who has shown us the way of salvation.

*The Deacon.*

Lord, bless us.

*The Priest.*

The Lord will bless you in His grace, now, henceforth, and for evermore.

*The Deacon reads the record of the dead.*

*The Priest bows and prays.*

XV. Give peace, O Sovereign Lord our God, to the souls of all who dwell in the tabernacles of Your saints. Graciously bestow upon them in Your kingdom Your promised blessing, which eye has not seen, and ear has not heard, nor has it entered into the heart of man what You, O God, have prepared for those who love Your holy name. Give peace to their souls, and deem them worthy of the kingdom of heaven.

Grant that we may end our lives as Christians, acceptable unto You and without sin, and be pleased to give us part and lot with all Your saints.

Accept, O God, by Your ministering archangels at Your holy, heavenly, and reasonable altar in the spacious heavens, the thank-offerings of those who offer sacrifice and oblation, and of those who desire to offer much or little, in secret or openly, but have it not to give.

Accept the thank-offerings of those who have presented them this day, as You accepted the gifts of Your righteous Abel:

*The Priest offers incense, and says: —*

As You accepted the sacrifice of our father Abraham, the incense of Zacharias, the alms of Cornelius, and the widow's two mites, accept also the thank-offerings of these, and give them for the things of time the things of eternity, and for the things of earth the things of heaven. Defend, O Lord, our most holy and blessed *Papas* Δ, whom You have fore-ordained to rule over Your Holy Catholic and Apostolic Church, and our most pious Bishop Δ, that they through many years of peace may, according to Your holy and blessed will, fulfil the sacred priesthood committed to their care, and dispense aright the word of truth.

Remember the orthodox bishops everywhere, the elders, deacons, sub-deacons, readers, singers, monks, virgins, widows, and laity.

Remember, O Lord, the holy city of our God, Jesus Christ; and the imperial city; and this city of ours, and all cities and all lands, and the peace and safety of those who dwell therein in the orthodox faith of Christ.

Be mindful, O Lord, of the return of the back-sliding, and of every Christian soul that is afflicted and oppressed, and in need of Your divine mercy and help.

Be mindful, O Lord, of our brethren in captivity. Grant that they may find mercy and compassion with those who have led them captive.

Be mindful also of us, O Lord, Your sinful and unworthy servants, and blot out our sins in Your goodness and mercy.

Be mindful also of me, Your lowly, sinful, and unworthy servant, and in Your mercy blot out my sins. Be with us, O Lord, who minister unto Your holy name.

Bless our meetings, O Lord.

Utterly uproot idolatry from the world.

Crush under our feet Satan, and all his wicked influence.

Humble now, as at all times, the enemies of Your Church.

Lay bare their pride.

Speedily show them their weakness.

Bring to naught the wicked plots they contrive against us.

Arise, O Lord, and let Your enemies be scattered, and let all who hate Your holy name be put to flight.

Bless a thousand times ten thousand Your faithful and orthodox people while they do Your holy will.

*The Deacon.*

Let those who are seated stand.

*The Priest says the following prayer:—*

Deliver the captive; rescue the distressed feed the hungry; comfort the faint-hearted, convert the erring; enlighten the darkened; raise the fallen; confirm the wavering; heal the sick; and guide them all, good Lord, into the way of salvation, and into Your sacred fold. Deliver us from our iniquities; protect and defend us at all times.

*The Deacon.*

Turn to the east.

*The Priest bows and prays.*

For You are far above all principality, and power, and might, and dominion, and every name that is named, not only in this world, but in that which is to come. Round You stand ten thousand times ten thousand, and thousands of thousands of holy angels and hosts of archangels; and Your two most honoured creatures, the many-eyed cherubim and the six-winged seraphim. With two they cover their faces, and with two they cover their feet, and with two they fly; and they cry one to another for ever with the voice of praise, and glorify You, O Lord, singing aloud the triumphal and thrice-holy hymn to Your great glory:—

Holy, holy, holy, Lord God of Sabaoth. Heaven and earth are full of Your glory.

*(Aloud.)*

You ever sanctify all men; but with all who glorify You, receive also, O Sovereign Lord, our sanctification, who with them celebrate Your praise, and say:—

*The People.*

Holy, holy, holy Lord.

*The Priest makes the sign of the cross over the sacred mysteries.*

XVI. For truly heaven and earth are full of Your glory, through the manifestation of our Lord and God and Saviour Jesus Christ. Fill, O God, this sacrifice with Your blessing, through the inspiration of Your all-holy Spirit. For the Lord Himself, our God and universal King, Christ Jesus, reclining at meat the same night on which He delivered Himself up for our sins and died in the flesh for all, took bread in His holy, pure, and immaculate hands, and lifting His eyes to His Father, our God, and the God of all, gave thanks; and when He had blessed, hallowed, and broken the bread, gave it to His holy and blessed disciples and apostles, saying:—

*(Aloud.)*

Take, eat.

*The Deacon.*

Pray earnestly.

*The Priest (aloud).*

For this is my body, which is broken for you, and divided for the remission of sins.

*The People.*

Amen.

*The Priest prays.*

After the same manner also, when He had supped, He took the cup of wine mingled with water, and lifting His eyes to You, His Father, our God, and the God of all, gave thanks; and when He had blessed and filled it with the Holy Spirit, gave it to His holy and blessed disciples and apostles, saying:—

*(Aloud.)*

Drink all of it.

*The Deacon.*

Pray earnestly again.

*The Priest (aloud).*

For this is my blood of the new testament which is shed for you and for many, and distributed among you for the remission of sins.

*The People.*

Amen.

*The Priest prays thus:—*

This do in remembrance of me; for as often as you eat this bread and drink this cup, you do show forth my death and acknowledge my resurrection and ascension until I come. O Sovereign and Almighty Lord, King of heaven, while we show forth the death of Your only-begotten Son, our Lord, God, and Saviour Jesus Christ, and acknowledge His blessed resurrection from the dead on the third day, we do also openly declare His ascension into heaven, and His sitting on the right hand of You, God and Father, and await His second terrible and dreadful coming, in which He will come to judge righteously the quick and the dead, and to render to each man according to his works.

XVII. O Lord our God, we have placed before You what is Yours from Your own mercies. We pray and beseech You, O good and merciful God, to send down from Your holy heaven, from the mansion You have prepared, and from Your infinite bosom, the Paraclete Himself, holy, powerful, and life-giving, the Spirit of truth, who spoke in the law, the apostles, and prophets; who is everywhere present, and fills all things, freely working sanctification in whom He will with Your good pleasure; one in His nature; manifold in His working; the fountain of divine blessing; of like substance with You, and proceeding from You; sitting with You on the throne of Your kingdom, and with Your only-begotten Son, our Lord and God and Saviour Jesus Christ. Send down upon us also and upon this bread and upon these chalices Your Holy Spirit, that by His all-powerful and divine influence He may sanctify and consecrate them, and make this bread the body.

*The People.*

Amen.

*The Priest (aloud).*

And this cup the blood of the new testament, of the very Lord, and God, and Saviour, and universal King Christ Jesus.

*The Deacon.*

Deacons, come down.

*The Priest (aloud).*

That to all of us who partake thereof they may tend unto faith, sobriety, healing, temperance, sanctification, the renewal of soul, body, and spirit, participation in the blessedness of eternal life and immortality, the glory of Your most holy name, and the remission of sins, that Your most holy, precious, and glorious name may be praised and glorified in this as in all things.

*The People.*

As it was and is.

*The Priest.*

XVIII. Peace be to all.

*The Deacon.*

Pray.

*The Priest prays in secret.*

O God of light, Father of life, Author of grace, Creator of worlds, Founder of knowledge, Giver of wisdom, Treasure of holiness, Teacher of pure prayers, Benefactor of our souls, who givest to the faint-hearted who put their trust in You those things into which the angels desire to look: O Sovereign Lord, who has brought us up from the depths of darkness to light, who has given us life from death, who has graciously bestowed upon us freedom from slavery, who has scattered the darkness of sin within us, through the presence of Your only-begotten Son, do Thou now also, through the visitation of Your all-holy Spirit, enlighten the eyes of our understanding, that we may partake without fear of condemnation of this heavenly and immortal food, and sanctify us wholly in soul, body, and spirit, that with Your holy disciples and apostles we may say this prayer to You: Our Father who art in heaven, etc.

*(Aloud.)*

And grant, O Sovereign Lord, in Your mercy, that we with freedom of speech, without fear of condemnation, with pure heart and enlightened soul, with face that is not ashamed, and with hollowed lips, may venture to call upon You, the holy God who art in heaven, as our Father, and say:—

*The People.*

Our Father who art in heaven, etc.

*The Priest prays: —*

Verily, Lord, Lord, lead us not into temptation, but deliver us from evil; for Your abundant mercy shows that we through our great infirmity are unable to resist it. Grant that we may find a way whereby we may be able to withstand temptation; for You have given us power to tread upon serpents, and scorpions, and all the power of the enemy.

*(Aloud.)*

For Yours is the kingdom and power.

*The People.*

Amen.

*The Priest.*

XIX. Peace be to all.

*The Deacon.*

Bow your heads to Jesus.

*The People.*

You, Lord.

*The Priest prays.*

O Sovereign and Almighty Lord, who sittest upon the cherubim, and art glorified by the seraphim; who has made the heaven out of waters, and adorned it with choirs of stars; who has placed an unbodied host of angels in the highest heavens to sing Your praise for ever; before You have we bowed our souls and bodies in token of our bondage. We beseech You to repel the dark assaults of sin from our understanding, and to gladden our minds with the divine radiance of Your Holy Spirit, that, filled with the knowledge of You, we may worthily partake of the mercies set before us, the pure body and precious blood of Your only-begotten Son, our Lord and God and Saviour Jesus Christ. Pardon all our sins in Your abundant and unsearchable goodness, through the grace, mercy, and love of Your only-begotten Son:

*(Aloud.)*

Through whom and with whom be glory and power to You, with the all-holy, good, and life-giving Spirit.

*The Priest.*

XX. Peace be to all.

*The Deacon.*

With the fear of God.

*The Priest prays.*

O holy, highest, awe-inspiring God, who dwellest among the saints, sanctify us by the word of Your grace and by the inspiration of Your all-holy Spirit; for You have said, O Lord our God, Be holy; for I am holy. O Word of God, past finding out, consubstantial and co-eternal with the Father and the Holy Spirit, and sharer of their sovereignty, accept the pure song which cherubim and seraphim, and the unworthy lips of Your sinful and unworthy servant, sing aloud.

*The People.*

Lord, have mercy; Lord, have mercy; Lord, have mercy.

*The Priest (aloud).*

Holy things for the holy.

*The People.*

One Father holy, one Son holy, one Spirit holy, in the unity of the Holy Spirit. Amen.

*The Deacon.*

For salvation and help.

*The Priest makes the sign of the cross upon the people, and says in a loud voice:—*

The Lord be with all.

*The Priest breaks the bread, and says:—*

Praise God.

*The Priest divides it among those present, and says:—*

The Lord will bless and help you through His great mercy.

*The Priest says:—*

Command.

*The Clergy say:—*

The Holy Spirit commands and sanctifies.

*The Priest.*

Lo, they are sanctified and consecrated.

*The Clergy.*

One holy Father, etc. (thrice).

*The Priest says:—*

The Lord be with all.

*The Clergy.*

And with your spirit.

*The Priest says:—*

The Lord Himself has blessed it.

*The Priest partakes, and prays.*

According to Your loving-kindness, etc.

*Or,*

As the hart pants after the water-brooks, etc.

*When he gives the bread to the clergy, he says:—*

The holy body.

*And when he gives the chalice, he says:—*

The precious blood of our Lord, and God, and Saviour.

# 4

*After the service is completed, the Deacon says:—*

XXI. Stand for prayer.

*The Priest.*

Peace be to all.

*The Deacon.*

Pray.

*The Priest says the prayer of thanksgiving.*

O Sovereign Lord our God, we thank You that we have partaken of Your holy, pure, immortal, and heavenly mysteries, which You have given for our good, and for the sanctification and salvation of our souls and bodies. We pray and beseech You, O Lord, to grant in Your good mercy, that by partaking of the holy body and precious blood of Your only-begotten Son, we may have faith that is not ashamed, love that is unfeigned, fullness of holiness, power to eschew evil and keep Your commandments, provision for eternal life, and an acceptable defence before the awful tribunal of Your Christ:

*In a loud voice.*

Through whom and with whom be glory and power to You, with Your all-holy, good, and life-giving Spirit.

*The Priest then turns to the people, and says:—*

XXII. O mightiest King, co-eternal with the Father, who by Your might has vanquished hell and trodden death under foot, who has bound the strong man, and by Your miraculous power and the enlightening radiance of Your unspeakable Godhead has raised Adam from the tomb, send forth Your invisible right hand, which is full of blessing, and bless us all.

Pity us, O Lord, and strengthen us by Your divine power.

Take away from us the sinful and wicked influence of carnal desire.

Let the light shine into our souls, and dispel the surrounding darkness of sin.

Unite us to the all-blessed assembly that is well-pleasing unto You; for through You and with You, all praise, honour, power, adoration, and thanksgiving are due unto the Father and the Holy Spirit, now, henceforth, and for evermore.

*The Deacon.*

Depart in peace:

*The People.*

In the name of the Lord.

*The Priest (aloud).*

---

XXIII. The love of God the Father; the grace of the Son, our Lord Jesus Christ; the communion and gift of the All-holy Spirit, be with us all, now, henceforth, and for evermore.

*The People.*

Amen. Blessed be the name of the Lord.

*The Priest prays in the sacristy, and says:—*

O Lord, You have given us sanctification by partaking of the all-holy body and precious blood of Your only-begotten Son; give us the grace and gift of the All-holy Spirit. Enable us to lead blameless lives; and guide us unto the perfect redemption, and adoption, and the everlasting joys of the world to come. For You are our sanctification, and we ascribe glory unto You, the Father, and the Son, and the All-holy Spirit, now, henceforth, and for evermore.

*The People.*

Amen.

*The Priest.*

Peace be to all.

*The People.*

And to your spirit.

*The Priest dismisses them, and says:—*

May God bless, who blesses and sanctifies, who defends and preserves us all through the partaking of His holy mysteries; and who is blessed forever. Amen.

www.ingramcontent.com/pod-product-compliance
Lightning Source LLC
Chambersburg PA
CBHW072144210225
22349CB00010B/936

\* 9 7 8 1 0 8 8 1 3 6 9 0 4 \*